Acknowledgment

I would like to express my heartfelt gratitude to all those who have contributed to the creation of this book on Exploring strategies to mitigate financial risks and build resilience. This project would not have been possible without the support, expertise, and dedication of numerous individuals, and it is with sincere appreciation that I acknowledge their contributions.

I extend my deepest thanks to my mentors, advisors, and subject matter experts who generously shared their insights, knowledge, and guidance throughout the process. Your expertise has been invaluable in shaping the content of this book and ensuring its accuracy and relevance.

I am grateful to the team of researchers, editors, and collaborators who tirelessly worked to gather information, conduct research, and refine the content. Your dedication to producing high-quality and comprehensive material is truly commendable.

I also extend my appreciation to the individuals and organizations that granted permission for the use of data, references, and resources. Your willingness to share valuable information has greatly enriched the content of this book.

My sincere thanks go to my family, friends, and loved ones who provided support, encouragement, and understanding throughout this journey. Your belief in me and your encouragement kept me motivated and focused.

I also extend my gratitude to the readers of this book. Your interest in exploring the complexities of risk management demonstrates a commitment to learning and growth. I hope that the insights shared within these pages will empower you to navigate uncertainties, make informed decisions, and embrace opportunities for a brighter future.

I appreciate you all.

Esther Campbell

Table of contents

Chapter 1

Understanding Risk

Risk is an inherent part of life, influencing decisions and outcomes in personal, professional, and societal contexts. Understanding risk is crucial for making informed choices, managing uncertainties, and minimizing potential negative consequences. This section of the book will delve into the fundamental concepts of risk, its different dimensions, and how it affects various aspects of our lives.

Defining Risk:

Begin by providing a clear definition of risk. Explain that risk refers to the probability of an event occurring and its potential impact, whether positive or negative. Emphasize that risk is not inherently negative; it can also present opportunities.

Types of Risk:

Introduce different categories of risk, such as financial risk, operational risk, strategic risk, reputational risk, legal risk, and more. Discuss how each type of risk manifests in different settings and the consequences it can bring.

Risk and Decision-Making:

Explore the relationship between risk and decision-making. Discuss how individuals and organizations assess risks when making choices and how risk perception can influence decisions.

Risk Tolerance and Appetite:

Explain the concepts of risk tolerance (the amount of risk one is willing to take) and risk appetite (the level of risk a person or organization is comfortable with). Describe how understanding one's risk tolerance can lead to better decision-making.

Risk vs. Reward:

Discuss the principle of risk versus reward, highlighting that higher potential rewards often come with higher levels of risk. Provide examples to illustrate this concept.

Probability and Impact:

Detail how risk is often assessed by evaluating both the probability of an event occurring and the potential impact if it does. Use practical scenarios to explain how these two factors interact.

Uncertainty and Variability:

Address the notion that uncertainty is an inherent part of risk. Discuss how variability and unpredictability contribute to the complexity of risk assessment.

Risk Assessment Tools:

Introduce various tools and methodologies used for risk assessment, such as risk matrices, probability distribution analysis, and scenario analysis. Explain how these tools aid in quantifying and prioritizing risks.

Risk Perception and Biases:

Explore how individuals perceive and react to risk differently based on cognitive biases and emotional factors.

Cultural and Societal Factors:

Highlight how cultural and societal factors can shape risk perceptions and attitudes. Provide examples of how different societies approach risk in various ways.

Economic and Social Impact:

Discuss how risks can have economic and social implications at both individual and societal levels. Explain how poorly managed risks can lead to financial crises, business failures, and other negative outcomes.

Chapter 2

Risk Assessment

Risk assessment is a systematic process used to identify, analyze, and evaluate potential risks in order to make informed decisions and implement appropriate risk management strategies. This section of the book will delve into the step-by-step approach to conducting risk assessments, the importance of thorough analysis, and practical techniques to assess and prioritize risks effectively.

Identifying Risks:

Begin by explaining the importance of identifying potential risks. Discuss how risks can stem from internal and external factors, including market trends, technological changes, operational processes, regulatory changes, and more.

Gathering Information:

Describe the process of gathering relevant data and information to identify potential risks. Emphasize the importance of collecting accurate and up-to-date information from various sources.

Risk Categorization:

Explain how categorizing risks can help streamline the assessment process. Discuss the benefits of categorizing risks into groups such as financial, operational, strategic, and reputational risks.

Risk Probability Assessment:

Detail the process of assessing the probability of each identified risk occurring. Provide guidance on how to use historical data, expert opinions, and statistical methods to estimate the likelihood of different events.

Risk Impact Assessment:

Explain how to evaluate the potential impact of each risk on the organization or individual. Discuss the factors to consider when assessing the severity of the consequences, including financial losses, operational disruptions, and reputational damage.

Quantitative and Qualitative Analysis:

Introduce the concepts of quantitative and qualitative risk analysis. Explain how quantitative analysis involves assigning numerical values to risks and their impact, while qualitative analysis focuses on assessing risks qualitatively based on their characteristics and potential outcomes.

Risk Ranking and Prioritization:

Describe how to rank and prioritize risks based on their probability and impact. Discuss methods such as risk matrices, risk scores, and risk heat maps to visually represent and prioritize risks.

Scenario Analysis:

Discuss how this technique helps in understanding the interconnectedness of risks and their potential cascading effects.

Sensitivity Analysis:

Introduce sensitivity analysis as a method to assess how changes in different variables or assumptions can impact the overall risk assessment. Highlight its importance in understanding the robustness of risk assessments.

Risk Assessment Tools and Software:

Mention the various tools and software available for conducting risk assessments, including specialized risk management software that can assist in data collection, analysis, and visualization.

Communication of Findings:

Stress the significance of effectively communicating the results of the risk assessment to relevant stakeholders. Explain how clear communication can aid in decision-making and the implementation of risk management strategies.

Chapter3

Risk Identification

Risk identification is a crucial step in the risk management process that involves systematically identifying potential risks that could impact an individual, organization, project, or endeavor. This section of the book will explore the methods, techniques, and best practices for effectively identifying risks and potential vulnerabilities.

Scope and Context:

Begin by emphasizing the importance of defining the scope and context of risk identification. Discuss how a clear understanding of the scope helps focus efforts on relevant areas and activities.

Stakeholder Involvement:

Explain how involving stakeholders with different perspectives can enhance the risk identification process. Discuss how individuals with various roles and expertise can contribute valuable insights.

Brainstorming and Creative Thinking:

Highlight the use of brainstorming sessions as a technique to generate a wide range of potential risks. Encourage creative thinking and an open environment where participants feel comfortable sharing their ideas.

Checklists and Templates:

Introduce the use of checklists, templates, and standardized risk registers to ensure a systematic approach to risk identification. Discuss how these tools can prompt individuals to consider risks across different categories.

Historical Data Analysis:

Explain the value of analyzing historical data and past experiences to identify recurring risks or patterns. Discuss how lessons learned from previous projects or incidents can inform current risk identification efforts.

SWOT Analysis:

Describe how conducting a SWOT (Strengths, Weaknesses, Opportunities, and Threats) analysis can help identify both internal and external risks. Explain how this technique aids in understanding an organization's current state and potential vulnerabilities.

Cause and Effect Analysis (Fishbone Diagram):
Introduce the cause-and-effect analysis, also known as the Fishbone or Ishikawa diagram. Explain how this visual tool helps identify potential causes and contributing factors that could lead to risks.

Expert Interviews and Surveys:
Discuss the importance of seeking input from subject-matter experts through interviews and

surveys. Explain how experts can provide valuable insights into risks related to their specific domains.

Benchmarking and Best Practices:

Explain how comparing the practices and experiences of similar organizations or projects can reveal potential risks that may have been overlooked.

Scenario Development:

Describe the process of creating hypothetical scenarios to explore various risk events and their potential consequences. Explain how this technique aids in uncovering risks that may not be immediately apparent.

Technological and Environmental Scanning:

Highlight the role of technology and environmental scanning in identifying emerging risks. Discuss how monitoring trends, technological advancements, and regulatory changes can help anticipate potential risks.

Risk Workshops:

Detail how risk workshops bring together stakeholders to collaboratively identify risks, share insights, and develop a comprehensive risk profile.

Chapter4

Risk Mitigation

Risk mitigation is the process of taking deliberate actions to reduce the likelihood or impact of identified risks. This section of the book will delve into the strategies, approaches, and best practices for effectively mitigating risks across various contexts, whether in personal, professional, or organizational settings.

Risk Mitigation Strategies:

Introduce the concept of risk mitigation and emphasize its importance in minimizing potential negative consequences. Discuss how risk mitigation strategies can vary based on the type of risk and the specific context.

Preventive Measures:

Detail preventive actions that can be taken to avoid or minimize the occurrence of potential risks. Discuss how early intervention and proactive planning can significantly reduce the likelihood of risks materializing.

Diversification:

Explain how diversifying resources, investments, or strategies can help spread risk and reduce the impact of a single risk event. Discuss its application in financial and business contexts.

Contingency Planning:

Describe the creation of contingency plans that outline specific actions to be taken if a risky event occurs. Discuss how these plans provide a roadmap for responding effectively and minimizing negative consequences.

Risk Transfer:

Explore the concept of risk transfer, where the responsibility for a risk is shifted to another party. Discuss mechanisms such as insurance, warranties, and contracts that facilitate risk transfer.

Hedging and Financial Instruments:

Introduce financial tools and instruments, such as options and futures, that can be used to hedge against financial risks, such as market fluctuations.

Redundancy and Backup Systems:

Explain how redundancy and backup systems can be implemented to ensure continuity of operations in the face of disruptions. Discuss their application in technology, infrastructure, and supply chain management.

Training and Skill Development:

Highlight the importance of training and skill development to mitigate risks related to human error or a lack of expertise. Discuss how investing in education and training can enhance preparedness.

Technology and Automation:

Discuss how technology and automation can reduce human involvement in high-risk processes, thereby minimizing the potential for errors and accidents.

Monitoring and Surveillance:

Explain how continuous monitoring and surveillance can help detect early signs of risky events. Discuss how data analytics and real-time monitoring contribute to timely risk mitigation.

Emergency Response Planning:

Detail the importance of developing comprehensive emergency response plans that outline steps to be taken during crisis situations. Discuss the role of simulations and drills in testing the effectiveness of these plans.

Communication and Transparency:

Emphasize the significance of open and transparent communication with stakeholders about potential risks and mitigation efforts. Discuss how effective communication can build trust and support.

Stakeholder Engagement:

Discuss how involving relevant stakeholders in risk mitigation efforts can lead to more effective solutions. Explain how collaboration can generate innovative approaches to risk reduction.

Chapter 5

Risk Transfer and Insurance

Insurance is one of the most common methods of risk transfer. This section of the book will explore the concepts of risk transfer, the role of insurance, types of insurance coverage, and best practices for effectively utilizing insurance to mitigate risks.

Understanding Risk Transfer:

Begin by explaining the concept of risk transfer, where the responsibility for a potential loss is transferred from one party to another. Emphasize that risk transfer does not eliminate the risk but shifts the financial impact.

Role of Insurance:

Introduce insurance as a mechanism for risk transfer. Explain how insurance policies provide financial protection against specific risks, with the insurer assuming the responsibility to compensate for losses.

Insurance Parties:

Describe the roles of the key parties in an insurance contract: the insured (policyholder), the insurer (insurance company), and the beneficiary (recipient of the insurance benefits).

Types of Insurance:

Discuss various types of insurance coverage, including:

Property Insurance: Protection against damage or loss of physical assets

Liability Insurance: Coverage for legal obligations arising from third-party claims

Health Insurance: Financial support for medical expenses and healthcare services

Auto insurance provides coverage for vehicle-related risks, including accidents and theft.

Business Interruption Insurance: Compensation for lost income due to business disruptions

Cyber Insurance: Protection against cyber-related risks and data breaches

Natural Disaster Insurance: Coverage for damage caused by natural catastrophes

Professional Liability Insurance: Coverage for professionals against errors and negligence claims

Premiums and Deductibles:

Explain how insurance policies involve the payment of premiums (regular payments) by the insured to the insurer. Describe deductibles as the portion of a claim the insured must pay before the insurance coverage kicks in.

Risk Assessment for Insurance:

Discuss how insurers assess risks before offering coverage. Explain that factors such as the type of coverage, the insured's risk profile, and the likelihood of claims influence premium costs.

Claims Process:

Detail the process of filing and processing insurance claims. Explain how the insured must provide evidence of the loss or damage to receive compensation.

Risk Management with Insurance:

Highlight how insurance is an integral part of an overall risk management strategy. Explain that insurance should complement other risk mitigation efforts and not be solely relied upon.

Selecting the Right Coverage

Provide guidance on how to select appropriate insurance coverage based on individual or organizational needs and risk exposures.

Limitations and Exclusions:

Discuss the limitations and exclusions of insurance policies. Explain that certain risks or circumstances may not be covered and may require additional coverage or alternative risk management strategies.

Insurance Market and Trends:

Briefly touch on the evolving landscape of the insurance industry, including emerging trends such as parametric insurance, peer-to-peer insurance, and technology-driven innovations.

Chapter 6

Crisis Management

Crisis management is the strategic process of preparing for, responding to, and recovering from significant and often unexpected events that have the potential to disrupt normal operations, harm an organization's reputation, or pose a threat to public safety. This section of the book will explore the key components of crisis management, including planning, response, communication, and recovery.

Understanding Crisis Management:
Begin by explaining the concept of crisis management and its importance in addressing and mitigating the impact of crises. Emphasize that

crises can take various forms, such as natural disasters, public health emergencies, technological failures, financial crises, and reputational threats.

Crisis Planning and Preparedness:

Describe the process of creating a comprehensive crisis management plan. Discuss how this plan outlines roles, responsibilities, and procedures to be followed before, during, and after a crisis. Emphasize the importance of regular training and drills to ensure preparedness.

Crisis Response:

Detail the steps involved in responding to a crisis. Explain the need for clear decision-making, quick actions, and coordination among relevant stakeholders. Discuss how a designated crisis management team plays a critical role in executing the response plan.

Communication Strategies:

Explore the importance of effective communication during a crisis. Discuss how timely and transparent communication with stakeholders, including employees, customers, partners, and the public, helps manage expectations and reduce confusion.

Crisis Communication Plan:

Explain the development of a crisis communication plan that outlines how information will be disseminated to various audiences. Discuss the use of   different   communication   channels, spokespersons, and messaging strategies.

Media Relations:

Describe the role of media relations in crisis management. Discuss the challenges of managing media inquiries and maintaining a positive public image during a crisis.

Stakeholder Engagement:

Emphasize the importance of engaging and collaborating with stakeholders, including government agencies, regulatory bodies, community leaders, and non-governmental organizations. Discuss how partnerships can enhance response and recovery efforts.

Resource Allocation:

Explain how crisis management involves effectively allocating resources such as personnel, equipment, and finances to address immediate needs and facilitate recovery.

Recovery and Rehabilitation:

Detail the process of recovery and rehabilitation after a crisis. Discuss how organizations must assess the extent of damage, restore operations, and implement measures to prevent future crises.

Learning and Continuous Improvement:

Discuss the post-crisis phase, where organizations reflect on the crisis management process.

Emphasize the importance of conducting a thorough post-crisis analysis to identify lessons learned and areas for improvement.

Case Studies:

Provide real-life examples of organizations that effectively managed crises and those that faced challenges. Analyze the strategies and approaches used in each case to highlight best practices and potential pitfalls.

Ethical Considerations:

Address the ethical dilemmas that may arise during a crisis. Discuss the importance of maintaining ethical standards and making morally sound decisions.

Chapter 7

Business Continuity Planning

Business continuity planning (BCP) is a comprehensive approach to ensuring an organization's ability to maintain essential functions, operations, and services during and after disruptive events. This section of the book will explore the key elements of business continuity planning, including risk assessment, recovery strategies, plan development, testing, and continuous improvement.

Introduction to Business Continuity Planning:
Begin by explaining the concept of business continuity planning and its significance in ensuring an organization's resilience against disruptions.

Emphasize that BCP aims to minimize downtime, protect assets, and enable a swift recovery.

Risk Assessment and Impact Analysis:

Describe the process of identifying potential risks and their potential impact on business operations. Discuss how a thorough risk assessment helps prioritize resources and develop targeted recovery strategies.

Business Impact Analysis (BIA):

Detail the role of the business impact analysis in quantifying the financial, operational, and reputational consequences of a disruption. Discuss how the BIA informs decision-making and resource allocation.

Recovery Strategies:

Explain the development of recovery strategies based on the identified risks and their impact. Discuss different strategies, such as maintaining redundant systems, outsourcing critical functions, and establishing backup sites.

Plan Development:

Describe the process of creating a business continuity plan that outlines step-by-step procedures to be followed in the event of a disruption. Discuss the importance of clear roles and responsibilities, contact information, and communication protocols.

Crisis Management Integration:

Discuss the integration of business continuity planning with crisis management efforts. Explain how BCP aligns with crisis response and communication strategies.

Communication and Notification:

Explore the role of effective communication in business continuity. Discuss how communication plans ensure that employees, stakeholders, and partners are informed during a disruption.

Testing and Exercises:

Detail the importance of regularly testing and exercising the business continuity plan. Discuss different testing methods, such as tabletop exercises and full-scale simulations, to validate the plan's effectiveness.

Training and Awareness:

Emphasize the need for training employees and stakeholders on their roles and responsibilities during a disruption. Discuss how raising awareness about BCP enhances preparedness.

Vendor and Supply Chain Resilience:

Explain how business continuity planning extends to vendors and suppliers. Discuss strategies to ensure the resilience of the supply chain and manage dependencies.

Technology and Data Recovery:

Discuss the role of technology in business continuity, including data backup, disaster recovery solutions, and IT infrastructure redundancy.

Document Management:

Detail the importance of maintaining up-to-date documentation, including the business continuity plan, recovery strategies, and contact information. Explain how documentation facilitates a coordinated response.

Regulatory Compliance and Legal Considerations:

Address how business continuity planning aligns with regulatory requirements and legal obligations.

Discuss the importance of understanding relevant regulations and industry standards.

Continuous Improvement:

Highlight the iterative nature of business continuity planning. Emphasize the need for regular reviews, updates, and enhancements to adapt to changing risks and organizational needs.

Chapter 8

Financial Risk Management

Financial risk management involves identifying, assessing, and mitigating risks that could impact an organization's financial stability, profitability, and value. This section of the book will explore the various types of financial risks, strategies for managing them, and the importance of effective risk management in financial decision-making.

Introduction to Financial Risk Management:
Begin by explaining the concept of financial risk management and its role in safeguarding an organization's financial health. Emphasize that financial risks arise from uncertainties in market

conditions, economic factors, and financial instruments.

Types of Financial Risks:

Discuss different types of financial risks, including:

Market Risk: Exposure to changes in market prices, such as interest rates, exchange rates, and commodity prices

Credit Risk: The risk of counterparty default or failure to fulfill financial obligations

Liquidity Risk: The risk of not being able to meet short-term financial obligations

Operational Risk: Risks arising from internal processes, systems, and human errors

Financial Fraud and Cyber Risk: Risks related to financial crime and cybersecurity breaches

Risk Assessment and Measurement:

Explain the process of assessing and measuring financial risks. Discuss methods such as value-at-risk (VaR), stress testing, and scenario analysis to quantify potential losses under different conditions.

Hedging and Derivatives:

Describe how organizations use financial derivatives (options, futures, and swaps) to hedge against market risks. Explain how derivatives can be used to lock in prices, mitigate interest rate risks, and manage currency exposure.

Diversification and Portfolio Management:

Discuss how diversification of investments can reduce overall risk by spreading investments across different assets. Explain portfolio management strategies to optimize risk-return trade-offs.

Credit Risk Management:

Explore strategies for managing credit risk, including conducting thorough credit assessments, setting credit limits, and monitoring the creditworthiness of counterparties.

Interest Rate Risk Management:

Explain how organizations manage interest rate risk through strategies such as interest rate swaps, forward rate agreements, and interest rate caps and floors.

Foreign Exchange Risk Management:

Detail techniques to manage foreign exchange risk, including currency hedging, forward contracts, and currency options.

Liquidity Risk Management:

Discuss the importance of maintaining sufficient liquidity to meet short-term financial obligations. Explain liquidity management strategies and stress testing to assess liquidity positions.

Regulatory Compliance and Reporting:

Address the regulatory environment surrounding financial risk management. Discuss the importance of complying with regulatory requirements and reporting obligations.

Risk Management Tools and Software:

Introduce risk management tools and software that assist in quantifying and managing financial risks. Discuss how technology can enhance risk assessment and decision-making.

Risk Management Culture:

Emphasize the importance of fostering a risk-aware culture within the organization. Discuss how leadership, communication, and employee engagement contribute to effective risk management.

Ethical Considerations:

Address ethical considerations in financial risk management, such as transparency, fairness, and avoiding conflicts of interest.

Chapter 9

Reputation Management

Reputation management is the strategic process of actively shaping, monitoring, and maintaining the perception and reputation of an individual, organization, brand, or entity among its stakeholders and the public. This section of the book will explore the significance of reputation, strategies for managing it, and the role of communication, transparency, and ethical considerations in maintaining a positive reputation.

Understanding Reputation Management:
Begin by explaining the concept of reputation management and its importance in building trust,

credibility, and goodwill. Emphasize that a positive reputation enhances an organization's ability to attract customers, partners, investors, and talented employees.

Components of Reputation

Discuss the multifaceted nature of reputation, encompassing factors such as quality of products and services, ethical practices, customer satisfaction, social responsibility, innovation, and employee well-being.

Reputation Assessment:

Detail the process of assessing an organization's current reputation. Discuss methods such as surveys, focus groups, online sentiment analysis, and media monitoring to gauge public perception.

Strategies for Reputation Management:
Explore different strategies for managing and enhancing reputation:

Proactive Engagement: Engaging with stakeholders through open communication, demonstrating commitment to values, and showcasing positive contributions to society

Crisis Preparedness: Developing crisis management plans to effectively address negative incidents and maintain trust during challenging times

Stakeholder Engagement: Building relationships with stakeholders, including customers, employees, investors, regulators, and the media

Transparency and Authenticity: Being transparent about operations, sharing successes and failures, and demonstrating authenticity in interactions

Social Responsibility: Engaging in socially responsible practices and supporting causes that align with the organization's values

Employee Advocacy: Empowering employees to become brand ambassadors and positive advocates

Online Reputation Management: Monitoring and managing online reviews, social media mentions, and digital content that influence perception

Crisis Communication and Reputation Repair:

Discuss how effective crisis communication is essential for reputation repair. Explain how acknowledging mistakes, taking responsibility, and implementing corrective actions can mitigate damage during crises.

Communication Channels and Platforms:

Address the use of various communication channels, including traditional media, social media, websites, and public relations, to shape and disseminate messages that positively impact reputation.

Ethical Considerations in Reputation Management:

Highlight the importance of ethical behavior in reputation management. Discuss how transparency, honesty, and integrity are crucial for building and maintaining a positive reputation.

Measuring Reputation:

Explain how reputation can be measured through key performance indicators (KPIs) such as customer loyalty, brand sentiment, media coverage, and stakeholder engagement.

Continuous Improvement and Adaptation:

Discuss the iterative nature of reputation management. Emphasize the need for ongoing assessment, adjustment of strategies, and staying attuned to changing stakeholder expectations.

Long-Term Value of Reputation:

Explore how a strong reputation contributes to long-term value creation, competitive advantage, and resilience against external challenges.

Chapter 10

Legal and Regulatory Compliance

Legal and regulatory compliance refers to the adherence of individuals, organizations, and entities to laws, regulations, and standards set forth by government authorities, industry bodies, and relevant governing bodies. This section of the book will explore the importance of compliance, the impact of non-compliance, strategies for achieving compliance, and the role of ethics in maintaining a strong compliance culture.

Introduction to Legal and Regulatory Compliance: Begin by explaining the concept of legal and regulatory compliance and its significance in ensuring that individuals and organizations operate within the boundaries of established laws and regulations. Emphasize that compliance is essential for maintaining trust, avoiding legal liabilities, and fostering a fair and just society.

Types of Compliance:

Discuss different categories of compliance, including:

Legal Compliance: Adhering to national, state, and local laws that govern various aspects of business and personal conduct

Regulatory Compliance: Following regulations set by governmental agencies and industry bodies that pertain to specific sectors or activities

Ethical Compliance: Upholding ethical principles and standards beyond legal requirements

Impact of Non-Compliance:

Detail the potential consequences of non-compliance, including legal penalties, fines, litigation, reputational damage, loss of business licenses, and harm to stakeholders.

Laws and Regulations:

Discuss common laws and regulations that impact businesses and individuals, such as labor laws, environmental regulations, data protection laws, anti-corruption laws, and industry-specific regulations.

Compliance Programs and Policies:

Explain how organizations develop and implement compliance programs and policies to ensure adherence to laws and regulations. Discuss the role of compliance officers and teams in monitoring and enforcing compliance.

Risk Assessment and Mitigation:

Describe the process of conducting risk assessments to identify potential compliance risks. Discuss strategies for mitigating these risks through preventive measures, internal controls, and ongoing monitoring.

Training and Education:

Emphasize the importance of educating employees and stakeholders about compliance requirements, ethical standards, and reporting mechanisms for potential violations.

Reporting and Whistleblower Protection:

Discuss the establishment of reporting channels and whistleblower protection mechanisms that allow employees to report potential violations without fear of retaliation.

Third-Party and Supply Chain Compliance:

Address the need for ensuring compliance throughout the supply chain and when dealing with third-party vendors, contractors, and partners.

International Compliance:

Explore the complexities of international compliance, including navigating different legal systems, cultural norms, and international treaties.

Technology and Data Privacy Compliance:

Discuss compliance with data protection and privacy regulations, including the handling of personal and sensitive data, cybersecurity measures, and data breach reporting.

Continuous Monitoring and Improvement:

Explain how compliance is an ongoing process that requires regular monitoring, review of policies, and adjustments to align with changing laws and regulations.

Ethics and Compliance Culture:

Address the integration of ethics into compliance efforts. Discuss how fostering an ethical culture promotes not only legal compliance but also responsible behavior and good corporate citizenship.

Chapter 11

Environmental and Social Risks

Environmental and social risks refer to potential adverse impacts on the environment and society that can result from the activities, operations, and decisions of individuals, organizations, and industries. This section of the book will explore the nature of environmental and social risks, their significance, strategies for identifying and mitigating them, and the role of sustainability and corporate social responsibility (CSR) in addressing these risks.

Introduction to Environmental and Social Risks:

Begin by explaining the concept of environmental and social risks and their importance in addressing sustainability challenges, protecting ecosystems, and promoting social well-being. Emphasize the interconnectedness between human activities and their impacts on the environment and society.

Types of Environmental Risks:

Discuss different types of environmental risks, including:

Pollution: Contamination of air, water, and soil by pollutants and harmful substances

Climate Change: Adverse effects resulting from greenhouse gas emissions and global warming

Biodiversity Loss: Impacts on ecosystems, species, and habitats due to human activities

Natural Resource Depletion: Overexploitation of finite resources such as water, minerals, and fossil fuels

Types of Social Risks:

Explore various types of social risks, including:

Human Rights Violations: Abuses of basic human rights, labor rights, and social justice

Community Displacement: Forced relocation of communities due to development projects

Labor Exploitation: Unfair labor practices, poor working conditions, and unsafe workplaces

Supply Chain Risks: Impacts on Suppliers, Workers, and Communities Throughout the Supply Chain

Impact and Consequences:

Detail the potential consequences of environmental and social risks, including harm to public health, ecosystem degradation, community unrest, legal liabilities, reputational damage, and regulatory sanctions.

Risk Identification and Assessment:

Explain how organizations identify and assess environmental and social risks through comprehensive risk assessments, stakeholder engagement, impact assessments, and materiality analyses.

Mitigation and Prevention Strategies:

Discuss strategies for mitigating environmental and social risks.

Environmental Management: Implementing sustainable practices, reducing emissions, waste management, and resource conservation

Social Responsibility: Ensuring Fair Labor Practices, Community Engagement, Human Rights Due Diligence, and Ethical Supply Chain Management

Climate Action: Setting emission reduction targets, adopting renewable energy sources, and integrating climate considerations into business decisions

Sustainability and CSR:

Explore the role of sustainability and corporate social responsibility in addressing environmental and social risks. Discuss how organizations can integrate responsible practices into their core business strategies.

Transparency and Reporting:

Address the importance of transparent reporting on environmental and social performance. Discuss sustainability reports, disclosures, and initiatives to communicate efforts and progress to stakeholders.

Engagement with Stakeholders:

Emphasize the significance of engaging with stakeholders, including communities, NGOs, regulatory authorities, and investors, to understand concerns, build trust, and collaboratively address risks.

Regulatory Compliance:

Explain how regulatory frameworks, international agreements, and industry standards play a role in addressing environmental and social risks. Discuss the legal obligations that organizations must adhere to.

Technological Innovation:

Highlight how technological advancements can contribute to mitigating environmental and social risks, such as clean energy technologies, sustainable agriculture practices, and circular economy solutions.

Ethics and Values:

Discuss the ethical considerations in addressing environmental and social risks. Emphasize the alignment of organizational values with responsible behavior and positive contributions to society.

Chapter 12

Supply Chain Risk Management

Supply chain risk management is the process of identifying, assessing, and mitigating potential risks that could disrupt the flow of goods, services, information, or finances within a supply chain. This section of the book will explore the significance of supply chain risk management, strategies for identifying and addressing risks, and the role of collaboration and resilience in ensuring a robust supply chain.

Introduction to Supply Chain Risk Management:

Begin by explaining the concept of supply chain risk management and its importance in ensuring the continuity, efficiency, and reliability of supply chain operations. Emphasize the interconnectedness of global supply chains and the potential impact of disruptions.

Types of Supply Chain Risks:

Discuss various types of supply chain risks, including:

Demand Risks: Fluctuations in customer demand, market changes, and demand forecasting errors

Supply Risks: Disruptions in raw material supply, production, distribution, and transportation

Operational Risks: Internal process failures, quality issues, and technology disruptions

Financial Risks: Currency fluctuations, credit risks, and financial instability of suppliers

Impact of Supply Chain Disruptions:

Detail the potential consequences of supply chain disruptions, including production delays, inventory shortages, increased costs, revenue loss, reputational damage, and customer dissatisfaction.

Risk Identification and Assessment:

Explain how organizations identify and assess supply chain risks through techniques such as risk mapping, scenario analysis, and vulnerability assessments.

Mitigation and Prevention Strategies:

Discuss strategies for mitigating supply chain risks.

Supplier Relationship Management: Developing strong relationships with key suppliers, conducting supplier audits, and assessing their risk profiles

Diversification: Reducing dependency on a single supplier or geographic region by diversifying sourcing and production

Inventory Management: Maintaining safety stock, buffer inventory, and agile inventory strategies to respond to unexpected disruptions

Demand Forecasting and Planning: Improving demand forecasting accuracy and aligning production with actual demand

Business Continuity Planning: Developing contingency plans and backup solutions to ensure supply chain resilience

Technology and Data Analytics:

Explore how technology, data analytics, and supply chain software can help monitor and manage supply chain risks. Discuss real-time visibility, predictive analytics, and digital platforms.

Collaboration and Communication:

Address the importance of collaboration and communication with suppliers, partners, and stakeholders. Discuss how information sharing and coordination can enhance supply chain resilience.

Supplier Risk Management:

Detail the process of assessing and managing risks associated with suppliers. Discuss supplier risk assessment tools, contractual agreements, and performance monitoring.

Global Supply Chain Risks:

Explore the challenges and considerations of managing risks in global supply chains, including geopolitical risks, trade disruptions, and regulatory changes.

Regulatory Compliance:

Discuss how regulatory compliance requirements impact supply chain operations, such as environmental regulations, labor standards, and product safety requirements.

Sustainability and Ethical Considerations:

Address the role of sustainability and ethical practices in supply chain risk management. Discuss responsible sourcing, fair labor practices, and environmental stewardship.

Continuous Improvement and Resilience:

Emphasize the iterative nature of supply chain risk management. Discuss the importance of continuous improvement, learning from disruptions, and building supply chain resilience.

Chapter 13

Decision-Making Under Uncertainty

Decision-making under uncertainty is the process of making choices or taking actions when the outcomes and consequences are not fully known due to incomplete information, ambiguity, and unpredictable future events. This section of the book will explore the challenges of decision-making under uncertainty, decision-making models, strategies for managing uncertainty, and the role of risk assessment and analysis.

Introduction to Decision-Making Under Uncertainty: Begin by explaining the concept of decision-making under uncertainty and its relevance in various aspects of life, business, and decision sciences. Emphasize that uncertainty arises from incomplete knowledge, unpredictable events, and ambiguity.

Challenges of Uncertainty:

Discuss the challenges posed by uncertainty, including the difficulty of predicting outcomes, the potential for unexpected risks, and the need to balance risks and rewards.

Decision-Making Models:

Introduce decision-making models that account for uncertainty:

Expected Utility Theory: Balancing potential outcomes by assigning probabilities and utilities to each scenario

Decision Trees: Visual representations of decision options, uncertain events, and potential outcomes

Monte Carlo Simulation: Using random sampling to model different scenarios and assess their probabilities and outcomes

Risk and Uncertainty Assessment:

Explain the importance of assessing and quantifying uncertainty and risk. Discuss methods such as sensitivity analysis, scenario analysis, and probabilistic modeling.

Strategies for Decision-Making Under Uncertainty:

Discuss strategies for making informed decisions despite uncertainty.

Minimax Regret: Choosing the option that minimizes the maximum potential regret

Maximin: Selecting the option that maximizes the minimum potential outcome

Bayesian Decision Theory: Incorporating prior knowledge and updating beliefs based on new information

Real Options Analysis: Incorporating flexibility to adapt decisions based on changing circumstances

Decision-Making in Business:

Explore how decision-making under uncertainty applies to business contexts, including investment decisions, product development, market entry, and resource allocation.

Emotional and Cognitive Factors:

Address the influence of emotions, biases, and cognitive limitations on decision-making under uncertainty. Discuss how overconfidence, loss aversion, and anchoring can impact choices.

Communication and Collaboration:

Emphasize the importance of effective communication and collaboration in decision-making. Discuss how diverse perspectives and expertise can enhance the assessment of uncertainty and options.

Ethical Considerations:

Discuss the ethical dimensions of decision-making under uncertainty, including transparency, accountability, and the potential consequences of decisions on stakeholders.

Decision Support Tools and Technology:
Explore how decision support tools, data analytics, and artificial intelligence can assist in assessing uncertainty, modeling scenarios, and recommending options.

Learning and Adaptation:
Address the iterative nature of decision-making under uncertainty. Discuss the value of learning from past decisions, feedback, and outcomes to improve future choices.

Long-Term Perspective:
Explain the importance of considering long-term implications when making decisions in the face of

uncertainty. Discuss the potential consequences of short-term focus and how to balance immediate gains with future risks.

Chapter 14

Risk Culture and Communication

Risk culture and communication play crucial roles in fostering a proactive and resilient approach to risk management within organizations. This section of the book will explore the concept of risk culture, the importance of effective risk communication, strategies for promoting a positive risk culture, and the role of leadership in shaping organizational attitudes toward risk.

Understanding Risk Culture:

Begin by explaining the concept of risk culture, which refers to the collective attitudes, values, beliefs, and behaviors of individuals within an organization regarding risk. Emphasize that risk culture influences how risks are perceived, communicated, and managed across all levels of the organization.

Importance of Risk Culture:

Discuss the significance of a strong risk culture in creating a resilient and risk-aware organization. Explain how a positive risk culture promotes transparency, accountability, ethical conduct, and informed decision-making.

Elements of Risk Culture:

Explore the key elements that contribute to a risk-aware culture:

Risk Awareness: Encouraging employees to recognize and understand various types of risks

Open Communication: Fostering an environment where employees feel comfortable discussing risks and concerns

Accountability: Holding individuals responsible for managing and mitigating risks in their areas of responsibility

Learning and Adaptation: Valuing lessons learned from past experiences and using them to improve risk management practices

Leadership: Setting the tone from the top by demonstrating a commitment to risk management and ethical behavior

Risk Communication:

Detail the role of effective risk communication in conveying information about risks to stakeholders, both internal and external. Discuss the challenges of clear and transparent risk communication.

Internal Risk Communication:

Discuss strategies for communicating risks within the organization, including:

Clear Messaging: Using simple and jargon-free language to convey risks and their potential impacts

Training and Education: Providing employees with the knowledge and skills to understand and manage risks

Reporting Mechanisms: Establishing channels for employees to report risks, concerns, and incidents

Scenario Planning: Using hypothetical scenarios to discuss potential risks and responses

External Risk Communication:

Address the importance of transparent communication with external stakeholders, such as customers, investors, regulators, and the public. Discuss the role of corporate social responsibility and sustainability reporting in external risk communication.

Strategies for Promoting a Positive Risk Culture:

Explore strategies for cultivating a positive risk culture:

Leadership Commitment: Leading by Example and Prioritizing Risk Management Efforts

Employee Engagement: Involving employees in risk identification, assessment, and mitigation

Incentives and Recognition: Recognizing and rewarding individuals who actively contribute to risk management efforts

Training and Development: Providing ongoing training to enhance risk awareness and management skills

Continuous Improvement: Encouraging a culture of continuous learning and adaptation in response to changing risks

Challenges and Obstacles:

Discuss potential challenges in promoting a positive risk culture, such as resistance to change, a lack of awareness, and conflicting priorities.

Ethical Considerations:

Address the ethical dimensions of risk culture and communication, including the importance of honesty, integrity, and responsible behavior in managing risks.

Chapter 15

Emotional Resilience

Emotional resilience, also known as psychological resilience, refers to an individual's capacity to effectively cope with and bounce back from adverse situations, stressors, challenges, and emotional experiences. This section of the book will explore the concept of emotional resilience, its importance for mental well-being, strategies for developing and enhancing resilience, and the role of self-care and support systems.

Understanding Emotional Resilience:
Begin by explaining the concept of emotional resilience as the ability to maintain emotional

well-being and mental strength in the face of life's ups and downs. Emphasize that emotional resilience does not eliminate difficulties but enables individuals to navigate them more effectively.

Components of Emotional Resilience:

Discuss the key components that contribute to emotional resilience:

Emotional Awareness: Recognizing and understanding one's emotions, thoughts, and reactions

Adaptability: Flexibly adjusting to changing circumstances and finding constructive ways to cope.

Problem-Solving: Developing effective strategies to address challenges and setbacks

Social Support: Building and maintaining relationships that provide emotional sustenance and encouragement

Positive Mindset: Cultivating a hopeful and optimistic outlook, even in the face of adversity

The Importance of Emotional Resilience:

Explore the significance of emotional resilience for mental health and overall well-being. Discuss how resilience enhances one's ability to manage stress, reduce the impact of negative emotions, and recover from emotional distress.

Strategies for Developing Emotional Resilience

Discuss practical strategies for developing and enhancing emotional resilience.

Self-Awareness: Reflecting on emotions, triggers, and patterns of response to build emotional intelligence

Mindfulness and Meditation: Practicing mindfulness to stay present, manage stress, and cultivate emotional balance

Cognitive Restructuring: Identifying and challenging negative thought patterns and replacing them with more constructive perspectives

Problem-Solving Skills: Developing effective problem-solving skills to address challenges and setbacks

Social Support: Building and nurturing relationships that provide empathy, understanding, and a sense of belonging

Stress Management: Engaging in stress-reduction techniques such as exercise, deep breathing, and relaxation

Goal Setting: Setting achievable goals and breaking them down into manageable steps

Humor and Positive Coping: Using humor and positive coping strategies to alleviate stress and enhance emotional well-being

Resilience in the Face of Adversity

Discuss real-life examples of individuals who have demonstrated remarkable emotional resilience in the face of significant challenges. Highlight the strategies they employed to overcome adversity.

Cultural and Contextual Factors:

Address how cultural, societal, and environmental factors can influence emotional resilience. Discuss the role of cultural norms, values, and social support systems.

Self-Care and Well-Being:

Explain the importance of self-care in maintaining emotional resilience. Discuss how self-care practices such as sleep, nutrition, exercise, and relaxation contribute to overall well-being.

Building a Supportive Environment:

Discuss the role of family, friends, mentors, and mental health professionals in providing a supportive environment for developing and maintaining emotional resilience.

Learning and Growth:

Emphasize the idea that setbacks and challenges can provide opportunities for learning, growth, and personal development. Discuss the concept of post-traumatic growth.

Chapter 16

Personal Risk Management

Personal risk management is the process of identifying, assessing, and mitigating potential risks that could impact an individual's financial security, well-being, and quality of life. This section of the book will explore the concept of personal risk management, the types of risks individuals face, strategies for managing those risks, and the role of insurance and financial planning.

Introduction to Personal Risk Management:

Begin by explaining the concept of personal risk management and its importance in safeguarding an individual's financial and personal well-being.

Emphasize that personal risk management aims to reduce the impact of unexpected events and uncertainties.

Types of Personal Risks:

Discuss various types of personal risks individuals may face, including:

Health Risks: Risks related to illness, injury, and medical expenses

Income Risks: Risks of job loss, reduced income, or disability

Property Risks: Risks of damage or loss to property, such as homes, vehicles, and personal belongings

Liability Risks: Risks of legal liability for injuries or damages caused to others

Longevity Risks: Risks associated with outliving retirement savings and income

Risk Assessment and Identification:

Explain the process of identifying and assessing personal risks. Discuss methods such as reviewing current financial circumstances, analyzing potential scenarios, and understanding individual and family needs.

Risk Mitigation Strategies:

Discuss strategies for mitigating personal risks.

Health and Wellness: Adopting a healthy lifestyle to reduce health risks and medical expenses

Emergency Fund: Building an emergency fund to cover unexpected expenses and provide a financial cushion

Insurance: Exploring different types of insurance, including health insurance, disability insurance, life insurance, homeowners and renters insurance, and liability insurance.

Income Protection: Consider income protection options such as disability insurance and unemployment insurance.

Asset Protection: Implementing measures to protect assets from property-related risks, such as home security systems and safe driving practices,

Estate Planning: Creating a comprehensive estate plan to ensure the smooth transfer of assets and minimize estate taxes

Financial Planning and Investments:

Discuss how effective financial planning can mitigate certain risks. Address concepts such as diversification, investment allocation, retirement planning, and managing inflation risk.

Insurance and Its Role:

Detail the role of insurance in personal risk management. Explain how insurance transfers the financial burden of potential losses to an insurance company.

Insurance Types:

Explore different types of insurance and their benefits:

Health Insurance: Protecting against medical expenses and healthcare costs.

Life Insurance: Ensuring financial security for dependents in the event of death

Property and Liability Insurance: Protecting against property damage, theft, and legal liability

Cost-Benefit Analysis:

Discuss the importance of conducting a cost-benefit analysis when considering insurance options. Address factors such as premiums, deductibles, coverage limits, and potential payouts.

Risk Tolerance and Goals:

Explain how an individual's risk tolerance and financial goals play a role in shaping their personal risk management strategy. Discuss the balance between risk-taking and risk avoidance.

Life Transitions:

Discuss how life transitions, such as marriage, parenthood, career changes, and retirement, can impact personal risk management needs and strategies.

By providing readers with a comprehensive understanding of personal risk management principles and practices, this section of the book equips them with the knowledge and tools needed to make informed decisions about their financial and personal well-being. It emphasizes the importance of proactive planning, risk assessment, and a balanced approach to managing risks to achieve long-term financial security and peace of mind.

Conclusion

The world we live in is characterized by constant change, uncertainty, and the potential for unexpected challenges. This book has delved into various aspects of risk and risk management, exploring how individuals, organizations, and societies can navigate these complexities to achieve resilience, success, and well-being.

From understanding different types of risks to implementing strategies for risk identification, assessment, and mitigation, it highlighted the significance of proactive risk management. The book explored risk culture, communication, and decision-making under uncertainty as essential components of building a foundation for effective risk management. Topics such as environmental and social risks, financial risk management, crisis management, and personal risk management have been examined to provide a comprehensive view of the risk landscape.

It's evident that risk is an inherent part of life and business, and addressing it requires a combination of knowledge, preparedness, adaptability, and collaboration. The above discussions have emphasized the importance of ethical considerations, transparency, and responsible practices in managing risks. After reading this book, you will understand that a proactive approach to risk management can lead to enhanced resilience, reputation, and long-term value creation.

As you navigate the dynamic and interconnected world of today and tomorrow, the principles and insights shared in this book serve as a guide for making informed decisions, embracing uncertainties, and cultivating a culture of resilience. By acknowledging risks, understanding their potential impacts, and employing effective strategies, you can work towards creating a safer, more stable, and more prosperous future for yourself and the generations to come. Remember, in the face of uncertainty, knowledge truly is power, and a proactive mindset can transform challenges into opportunities for growth and success.

www.ingramcontent.com/pod-product-compliance
Lightning Source LLC
Chambersburg PA
CBHW062330290526
45794CB00005B/1973